POEMS ALOUD

WIDE EYED EDITIONS

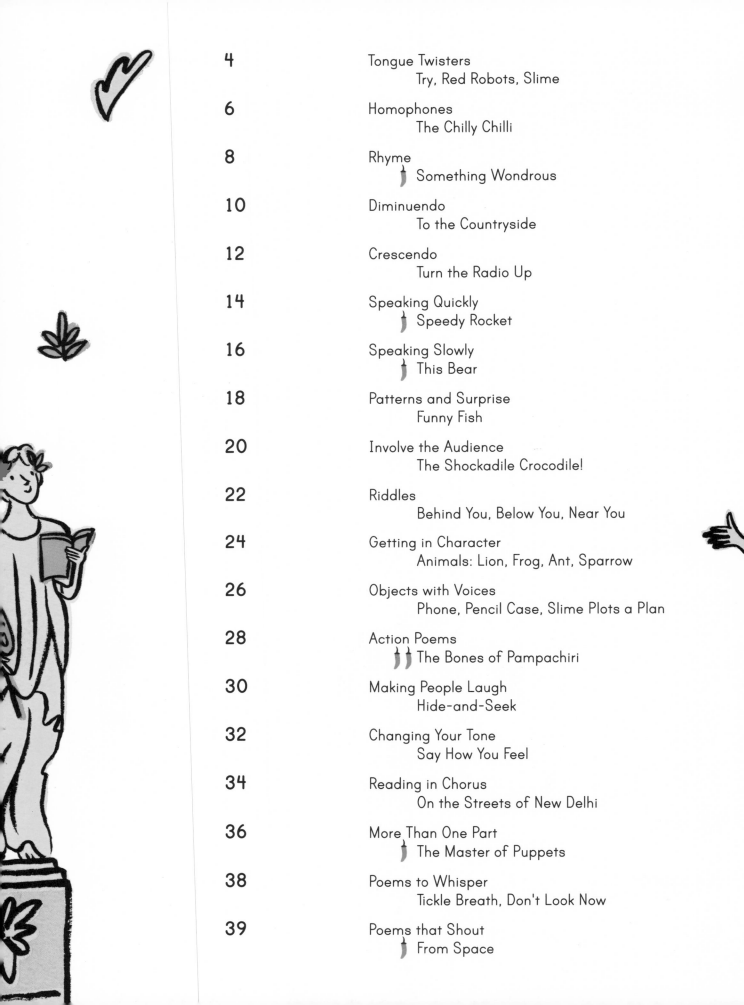

INTRODUCTION

POEMS ARE MADE TO BE PERFORMED!

We get the word 'lyrics' from the fact that poetry used to be read aloud to the music of a stringed instrument called a lyre. Poetry and performance have always gone hand in hand and here you will find a selection of poems to help you perfect your performance skills. Learn to use your voice like an instrument, and whip out your acting skills and make your audience laugh! Some of these poems are 'hot', meaning they might have some difficult words or deal with some complicated themes – we've put some chilli signs next to these ones so that you can work your way up to them.

🌶 = HOT!

🌶🌶 = EXTRA HOT!

There are poems here for you to perform alone, with friends and in large groups but however you perform them remember the biggest rule of all, poetry is fun and ultimately there are no rules! You can shout a poem intended to be whispered, read a group poem by yourself or add actions to a tongue twister. All the special techniques are here to help you and give you ideas of different ways of approaching a poem. Once you have tried them all you will have experienced a ton of performance techniques that you can mix up and dip into whenever you want. So let's get started – jump in and start performing your poems **ALOUD!**

TONGUE TWISTERS

are a wonderful way to improve your diction
(how clearly you can say words). Make sure
every word is powerful and is heard.

TRY

Try twisting your tongue
then tuning your teeth,
try taking your tonsils
from a tummy tickling thief.

Try tasting your tears
then trumpeting your toes,
try taping your temper
to the tip of your nose.

RED ROBOTS

Red robots are on the rise,
grasping their red, radiating bellies.
Red robots have red eyes
and red rust on their radio relays.

Red robots race on rails
repurposed from railways.
Red robots are revolutionary
with their radioactive rays.

THE SLIME TAKEOVER

Slipping, shimmering, stinking slime,
sloppy cerise or shades of scarlet sublime.
It sticks and sucks and spits and spools,
snaking slime slumping several school walls.
The slime swells, and stretches, and starts to sprout,
sliming several school halls as students scream and shout.
"Scary Slime Subsumes Schools",
say a slew of scandal sheets.
Their swan song headline
as the slime swallows scores of the city's streets.

THE CHILLY CHILLI

Some words sound the same as each other but mean different things.
These are homophones. You can make the meaning clear from the context.
Try emphasising the homophones in **bold** as you read.

A chilli pepper was picked,
packed and shipped to store,
popped into a fridge,
(a **frigid**, frosted **fridge**),
where it felt a little chilly.

A little **chilly chilli**
feeling cold and in a **knot**.
Not a happy, chilly chilli.
In fact, this chilli feels quite ill
like it's caught the **flu**.
It **flew** all this way
packed into a **plane**
to add heat to otherwise **plain** food.

The chilli **meets** the **meats**
that sit stacked in the fridge
and tells them where it's **been**,
as it describes its sun-soaked past
the chilled baked-**beans** start to dream.

So now the fridge is filled
with foods attentively listening,
imagining the sun-streaked **blue** skies
under which the chilli grew,
about the warm winds
that **blew** through the chilli's leaves.

And from hearing the story
the foods can feel the warm **weather**
whether they've been abroad or not.
They're there as they listen,
no longer **tied** to their cold reality
they imagine the rolling **tide**
they **see** the **sea**.
They tell their daughters and **sons**
of a **sun** that warms
with a light that never buzzes.
The **chilly chilli's** story
sets them free.

YOGHURT

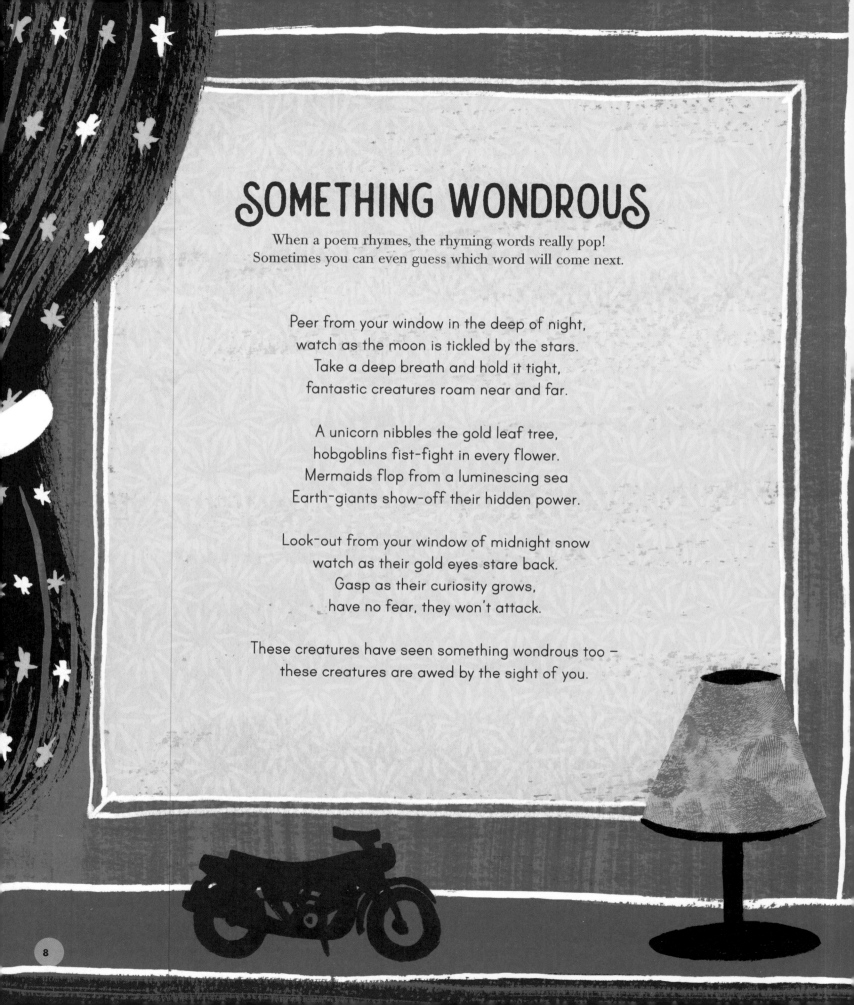

SOMETHING WONDROUS

When a poem rhymes, the rhyming words really pop!
Sometimes you can even guess which word will come next.

Peer from your window in the deep of night,
watch as the moon is tickled by the stars.
Take a deep breath and hold it tight,
fantastic creatures roam near and far.

A unicorn nibbles the gold leaf tree,
hobgoblins fist-fight in every flower.
Mermaids flop from a luminescing sea
Earth-giants show-off their hidden power.

Look-out from your window of midnight snow
watch as their gold eyes stare back.
Gasp as their curiosity grows,
have no fear, they won't attack.

These creatures have seen something wondrous too –
these creatures are awed by the sight of you.

TO THE COUNTRYSIDE

Try and use your voice like an instrument going from loud to quiet.
This effect is called diminuendo.

THE BEEPING OF THE TRAFFIC
BEEPBEEPBEEP!
Roars in our ears.

THE BELCHING OF THE FACTORIES
CLUNKCLUNKCLUNK!
Shudders in our ears.

THE HUFFING OF THE PEOPLE
HUFFHUFFHUFF!
Mumbles in our ears.

As we leave
the roaring, shuddering, mumbling city
behind us.

The whizz of the motorway cars
weee-ooowww-weee-ooowww-weee-ooowww
hums in our ears.

The whoosh of crops in the field
swish-swish-swish
plays in our ears.

The pebble-roll of the sea on the shore
hushes in our ears.

As we play the hum of hushes of...
noise no more
noise   no   more
noise   no   more
in the countryside.

TURN THE RADIO UP

Start softly and finish LOUD. This is called crescendo!

Tiny click of the volume knob
to turn the radio on.
A hiss of whispered static,
I can hardly hear my song.

So I readjust the tuning
until my song's a little clearer,
it's just above a whisper
so I move a little nearer.

The clicking of the volume knob
turns my song into a SHOUT!
The thrumming of the bass
I can easily make-out...
    twang
      twang
        twang.
So I click a little louder
until my song becomes a riot,
the drums vibrating through my body
and my body really likes it...
    Boom
      boom
        boom.

Now come the vocals
and I really love this bit,
so click up the treble
this is the real... deal!

And now my song is singing,
voice a booming mass of sound,
I start to join in,
I imagine I'm roaring to a crowd.
I'm screaming down a microphone,
I am the ocean's throat.
I'm clapping out the rhythm
I'm a-banging with my boot,
I'm bellowing the low bit,
I make hurricanes sound mute.

Now the crowd is within me,
painting the largest sound you've ever seen,
a wall of ear-splitting symphony,
a vocal Godzilla scene!

We are a screeching melody,
thumping reverberations.
We are louder than crashing planets
we are the thunderous cry of constellations.

SPEEDY ROCKET

This poem is a race.
Read as fast and as clearly as you can. GO!

This rocket's going fast!
Super-fast!
Faster than light,
it's out of sight!
A zipping zapping rocket
on a slip stream trip.
It rides
it rips
through the Milkyway it dips.
It whips,
it slips,
meteors it clips!

It zips,
it tips,
this rocket shakes its hips!

This super-duper-blooper rocket
sliding on a beam of light,
it's bright, a fright, it swerves incredibly tight.
This rocket's so wonderfully fast,
It arrives at night time before night!

It's a dream-exploding,
mind-imploding,
zooming melody of thought-dissolving,
whizzing cacophony of engine thrust
and time revolving!
An incredible super-speedy rocket ship!

THIS BEAR

Some poems sound best when read slowly.
Take your time, pause and breathe to add emphasis.

This lumbering bear is old.
This lumbering, bumbling bear
has shuffled over rugged
imagined mountains.
Urged his bulk, slow and strong.
Slow as geography.
Strong as tree growth
through the forests of his mind.

This hulking brown bear
furred in shag pile.
Cloaked in dusty winter coats,
sways to the tune
of the camera flash.
Eyebrows worn smooth,
his back is bald from sitting.

This ungainly bear
takes two dreamy steps
from a cage bathed
in decades of eyebrow fur,
rusted with blood specks.
He swaddles out to the first
deep earth beneath his paws,
the first thick wind through his thick fur
as his seasoned desires of water and wood
and grass and stone
roll out the colour of his imaginings.

This heavy bear,
this happy bear,
this home bear.
Sighs out to freedom.

FUNNY FISH

Some poems create suspense and comedy through structure. There are a
lot of rhymes in this poem… sea, be, me, body. As you read, emphasise the rhyme
so that when you get to "Dinner" the audience are in for a nice surprise!

I live in the sea,
I'm as sweet as can be,
I'm a tiny little clown fish
but please don't stare at me.

I'm tiny and pretty,
colours all around my body,
a beautiful little clown fish
living by a sea anemone.

I have no enemies,
I'm dressed to please, you see,
a wonderfully fashionable clown fish
with a flair for modesty.

Here comes one to admire me,
a handsome princely fishy
who appreciates a pretty clown fish,
what has he got for me?

His smile is so deadly,
a handsome catch for me,
just a modest pretty clown fish
by her sea anemone.

He wants to speak to me,
his lips part so slowly,
I'm a giddy, pretty clown fish.
What will he say to me?

"Please swim to me,
I find your anemone so stingy!
Delicious little clown fish,
I'm not your enemy."

I feel a little silly
swimming to this handsome beasty,
but he loves this little clown fish,
I'm a stripy beauty.

"My little fish finger swim closer to me,
My darling fish cake from the bottom of the sea,
my scrumptious little clown fish
you are the one for... DINNER!"

"Get into my tummy
I want you for my tea,
vainglorious little clown fish
you're the treat for me."

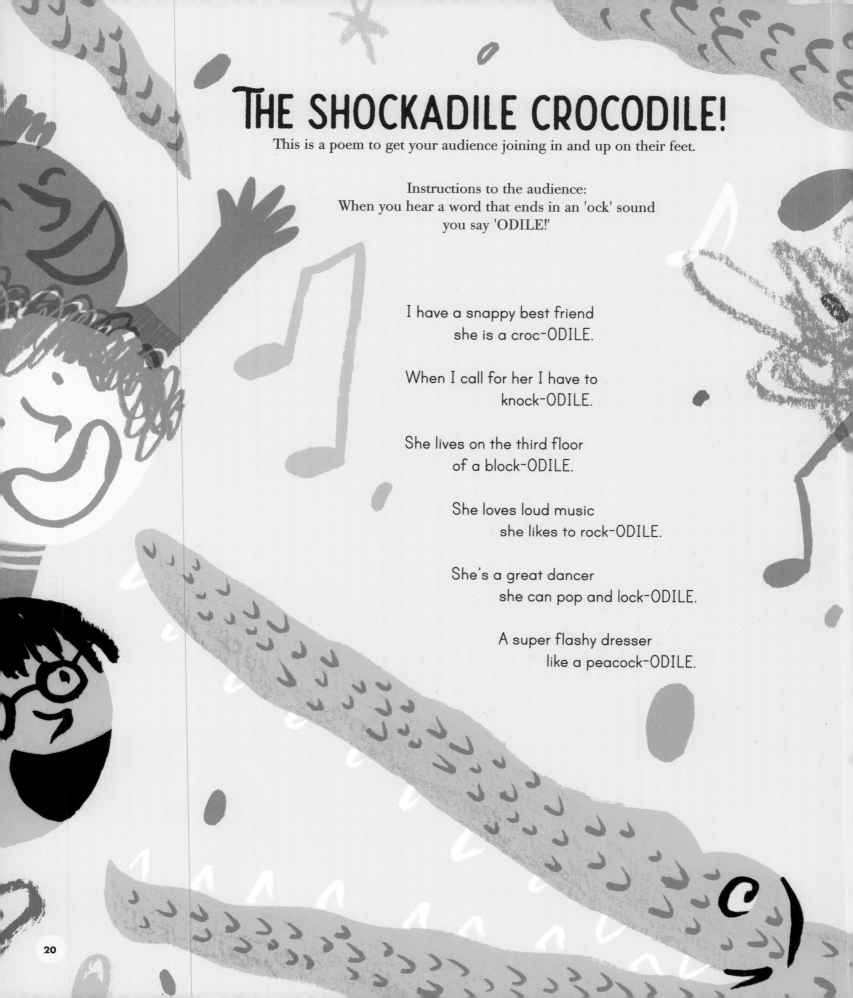

THE SHOCKADILE CROCODILE!

This is a poem to get your audience joining in and up on their feet.

Instructions to the audience:
When you hear a word that ends in an 'ock' sound
you say 'ODILE!'

I have a snappy best friend
she is a croc-ODILE.

When I call for her I have to
knock-ODILE.

She lives on the third floor
of a block-ODILE.

She loves loud music
she likes to rock-ODILE.

She's a great dancer
she can pop and lock-ODILE.

A super flashy dresser
like a peacock-ODILE.

She has amazing patterns
on her sock-ODILES.

She won't be caught dead wearing
a frock-ODILE.

She does what she wants
she is a shock-ODILE.

My incredible best friend
is a shock-ODILE,
frock-ODILE,
sock-ODILE,
peacock-ODILE,
lock-ODILE,
rock-ODILE,
block-ODILE,
knock-ODILE
CROCODILE!

RIDDLES

These tricky riddles put your audience to the test. Will they work out the answer from your clues? Speak slowly and carefully and repeat your riddle if necessary.

BEHIND YOU

I'm always behind you
very rarely in front
except when I go travelling.
I eat your lunch before you do.
I've seen all your books.
Whatever you give me
I'll make sure no one else will take a look.

BELOW YOU

I often stink,
but have a soul (sort of)
I keep you knotted
so you never trip.
When you run
I help you get a grip.

NEAR YOU

I'm clear when I'm empty,
see-through when I'm full.
My insides taste of nothing,
yet you want me.
Need me!
I'm full of leaks and gulps.
My brothers choke the oceans.

*Backpack **Trainer ***Water Bottle

ANIMALS

Try and think like the creature whose story you are telling. Imagine how these animals would speak if they could and use this voice to read their poem.

LION

I am meat-licker,
bone-cruncher,
big-meower.
I cat-walk with pride.
My mane is a hairdo of envy.
My roar is a rumble of mountains.
My claws, a savannah of pain.

FROG

I leap, I croak
I am the friend of witches.
I hop, I leap
I'm often found in ditches,
in ponds,
in lakes
and even under logs,
some say I'm green and warty
but I'm a smooth, jewel-skinned frog.

ANT

I'm so small.
I'm sooooo small.
I'm sooooooo very teeny, tiny small.

But I am MANY.
I am colony.
I am jaw and acid spit and attack and bite
and weight lifter,
I am Red and Black and Fire and Crazy and Bullet.

SPARROW

Me tweet. Me hop.
Me peck!
Peck, peck peck.
Me ruffle feather – dust bath.
Me flee.
Me swoop and dive.
Me tweet and chirp
and peck, peck, peck.

OBJECTS WITH VOICES

Imagine what it would be like if objects could talk.
Try and imagine how they would feel and how they would speak.
When we imagine objects as people, it is called personification.

PHONE

Stop shouting at me!
You really know how to press my buttons!
You're a noisy stink breath.
A constant giggle tummy-tickler.
My home in your pocket
dials up my anger.
You make me vibrate with fury.

PENCIL CASE

I love holding your dreamer markers,
your thought spinners,
the soft rubbed corners
of your mistakes
and the inks of your wins.
I adore the notes you give me for safe keeping,
the messages from friends,
the saved sweet.
I am happy to hold
the edge of your sharpener,
pleased to help you define
your best ideas.

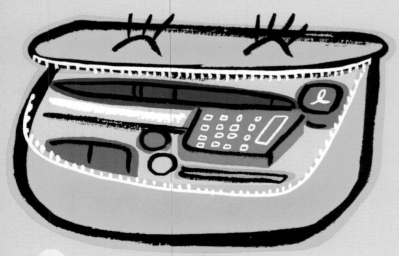

SLIME PLOTS A PLAN

I'm waiting as I wobble...
plotting as I plop!
Determined to get all the young people
to make my slippery brothers and sisters –
in pink and blue,
purple and green,
with sparkles and neon.
For one day, soon,
all us slimes
will combine
TO TAKE OVER THE WORLD.

THE BONES OF PAMPACHIRI

Try and bring this poem to life by acting out the verbs as you read
them out. Verbs are 'doing words' such as climb and fall.

As I journeyed through the highlands
of the thin-aired peaks of Peru,
I discovered something sinister,
never-seen and totally new.

And as I swatted the buzz
of the blood-sucking flies,
and stepped over the scorpions
and the black widow's venomous eye.

I scrambled up the yellow rocks
slipped,
dangled and nearly fell!
I kept up my climb
what would my story tell?

The sun was getting higher
burning pain into my skin,
I clambered the zig-zags of the ridge backed crags,
my marrow feeling thin.

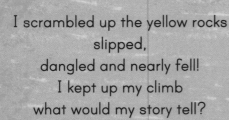

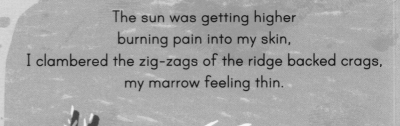

I darted through the cacti
where the dead-eye goats bleat,
I rested by a sun-soaked rock,
removed cacti spines from my feet.

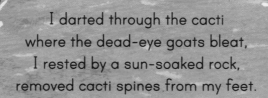

The cavern was more mouth than rock,
its entrance baring teeth.
As I crept nearer
I felt a welcome wave of ill-got relief.

I gasped at the site of the cavern
that grinned at the peak.
Their shaded depths a threatening relief
for my burnt skin and aching feet.

For they were not teeth,
my sweat abated then pooled onto the floor.
For they were not giant molars or incisors,
but instead skeletons, that littered the floor.

Skeletons in this sun-fractured valley,
skeletons of every age and height –
the bones all looked ancient
but something else was not right.

The skulls of these skeletons
were long and misshaped,
their craniums terribly domed at the peak
my mind started to quake.

I ran from the mountain,
tripped and bled and tumbled,
took no notice of the cacti
or the clouds that started to rumble.

My legs a blur of fleeing,
my heart an ossified thump,
I stumbled into the town of Pampachiri
a bruised and terrified lump.

29

HIDE-AND-SEEK

Here's a poem to make your audience laugh. Comedy is all about timing and expression. Try it out on a few friends and see which parts make them laugh the most and then emphasise those parts.

Me and my sister
always play-hide-and seek.
She hides in the garden
between the pumpkins.
I hide in the wardrobe
between mum's dresses.
She hides in the front-room
behind the sofa.
I hide in the bath
behind the shower curtain.

But we're not very good at hiding.

I find her in the garden
with a pumpkin on her head.
She finds me in the wardrobe
in a pile of mum's dresses.
I find her in the front-room
feet sticking out from behind the sofa.
She finds me in the bathroom
soaking wet and laughing.

SAY HOW YOU FEEL

The emotion in your voice helps the audience know how
the poem should make them feel. Change your tone and try and
show your different emotions as you read these poems.

When I'm sad
it feels like the sky is crashing down,
like the oceans are rising
and the ground is swallowing me up.
All is dark and cold.

When I'm nervous
it feels like my heart
is going to lightning-strike out of my chest,
like my skin is raining,
like my belly is a mudslide.

When I'm happy
my cheeks feel like rose buds,
my tummy glows with sunlight,
my shoulders are a forest breeze.

When I'm angry
my body is rock,
my face is wet clay.
Meteorites inhabit my fists,
my voice is all smoke and fire.

When I'm excited
my toes are ants,
I'm a river bubbling
and an air current of wishes,
my smile could explode the sun.

ON THE STREETS OF NEW DELHI

In ancient Greece groups of people performed
poems together and they were called choruses.
In your chorus, try reading some lines
as a group and some lines on your own.

On the streets of New Delhi
a small brown dog yawns.
The morning light is golden
on the new streets of barking New Delhi.

On the streets of New Delhi
an okra seller calls.
With okra as green as grasshopper legs
on the new streets of barking, selling New Delhi.

BARK

BARK

CHEEP

CHEEP

34

HE HE

HE HE

On the streets of New Delhi
a tuk-tuk tarries on a dusty road
thrumming its song
on the new streets of barking, selling, thrumming New Delhi.

On the streets of New Delhi
children giggle in starched school uniforms
chuckling their studies
on the new streets of barking, selling, thrumming, chuckling New Delhi.

TUK

TUK

CAW

THE MASTER OF PUPPETS

Create characters by giving each performer a
different puppet to bring to life with their voice.

PERSON 1

The first puppet was a blur of spinning
as it tumbled onto the stage
its strings unravelling
from the unseen puppet master above.

PERSON 2

I am a puppet of grace
dressed in a dress of obsession
all thrills and wows
all silk and swoosh
I glide over the stage
in a dance of captivation.

PERSON 1

The second puppet
crashed down
strings a mess of webs
dangled and tangled
from the unseen puppet master above.

PERSON 3

I am a puppet of confusion
a clown of falls and trips
wreathed in well-worn wonders
of harlequin diamonds
and baggy trousers.
I somersault to the clap.

PERSON 1

The third puppet
slips down its own strings
smooth and restrained
leaving nothing to chance
keeping a tension in its connection
with the unseen puppet master above.

PERSON 4

I am a puppet of perfection
slick and considered
tailored in black
stitched in quality
I slink through the spotlights
my heels tapping.

PERSON 1

Now the strings are lowering –
the puppet master coming into view
a threaded face of frowns
a knotted expression
a master of fraying possibilities...
A master formed
of our tangled connections...
We are the seen puppet master.

POEMS TO WHISPER

When you are performing, your audience can be lots of people, or just one.
Try whispering these poems in a friend's ear.

TICKLE BREATH

My breath in your ear may delight and tickle
may make you squirm, and laugh and wiggle
as I get uncomfortably near.

But I have something lovely to say
a little thought to brighten your day.
Your smile makes everyone cheer.

DON'T LOOK NOW

Don't look now
don't move, don't breathe
there's something behind you
unlike anything I've seen
it's looking
right at you
eyes hollow as night
it's pointing its long fingers.
Its mouth wants to bite.
It's moving its grey lips
so horribly slow
the words it is saying
are whispered and low.
Don't look now
it's incredibly near
don't move a hair's width,
It's whispering in your ear.

POEMS THAT SHOUT

Each word in a poem is special, and people listen to them carefully. That is why if you have an important message to tell, a poem is a good way to say it and get your message across loud and clear.

FROM SPACE

Seen from space
our planet is
a blue marble,
tiny and vulnerable,
a child's plaything.

When giants play at marbles
the marbles often crack.
A crack for all the plastic
clogging up the seas.
A crack for all the pollution,
a crack for the felling of trees.
A crack for all the oil
that spills and coats and chokes,
a crack for every politician
who says global warming's a joke.

Seen from space
our planet is
a teary eye,
sad and soft,
begging to be wiped.

When tears are left to pool
sadness drowns us all...
A tear for the crops
that can no longer flourish and grow.
A tear for every child
who will never get to grow old.
A tear for every bullet,
every bomb
that should have never been made.
A tear for the next generation
who never asked to play this game.

Given a little space,
could the planet heal?

Space for the fish
to repopulate the seas.
Space for the forests
to once again know trees.
Space for the skies to cry away the smoke.
Space for the next generation
to fix what their forefathers broke.

For my very noisy nieces and nephews - D.G-B.

Poems Aloud © 2020 Quarto Publishing plc.
Text © 2020 Joseph Coelho.
Illustrations © 2020 Daniel Gray-Barnett

First published in 2020 by Wide Eyed Editions.
First published in paperback in 2022 by Wide Eyed Editions, an imprint of The Quarto Group.
1 Triptych Place, 2nd Floor, London, SE1 9SH, United Kingdom.
T (0)20 7700 6700 F (0)20 7700 8066 **www.Quarto.com**

A catalogue record for this book is available from the British Library.

ISBN 978-0-7112-6392-5

The illustrations were created with traditional and digital media
Set in Nature Spirit, Bodoni and Print Clearly

Published by Georgia Amson-Bradshaw
Designed by Myrto Dimitrakoulia
Edited by Lucy Brownridge
Production by Dawn Cameron

Manufactured in Guangdong, China TT052023

9 8 7 6 5 4